Is Kristen Ulmer out of her mind?
You might think so
when she describes some of the jumps
she has made on skis.
For instance, there was the time
she flew through the air so out of control
that she fainted from fear.
Luckily, she didn't kill herself.
But she did crash into a tree.

Still, Ulmer didn't stop skiing.
Instead, she went out
looking for even bigger jumps.

A skier struggles to control a jump.

skiing the Impossible

Henry Billings and Melissa Billings

Published in association with The Basic Skills Agency

Hodder & Stoughton

A MEMBER OF THE HODDER HEADLINE GROUP

Acknowledgements

Cover: Karl Weatherly/Corbis.

Photos: pp. 1, 5, 9, 23 Action-Plus Photographic; p. 12 Corbis; p. 19 © Allsport;
p. 26 Associated Press/Bozeman Daily Chronicle.

Orders: please contact Bookpoint Ltd,130 Milton Park, Abingdon, Oxon OX14 4SB. Telephone: (44)
01235 827720. Fax: (44) 01235 400454. Lines are open from 9.00–6.00, Monday to Saturday, with a
24 hour message answering service. Email address: orders@bookpoint.co.uk

British Library Cataloguing in Publication Data
A catalogue record for this title is available from The British Library

ISBN 0 340 74778 1

Published by Jamestown Publishers,
a division of NTC/Contemporary Publishing Group, Inc.

First published in UK 1999 by Hodder & Stoughton Educational Publishers
Impression number   10 9 8 7 6 5 4 3
Year   2004 2003 2002

Typeset by Fakenham Photosetting Ltd, Fakenham, Norfolk.
Printed in Great Britain for Hodder & Stoughton Educational, a division of Hodder Headline Plc, 338
Euston Road, London NW1 3BH by The Bath Press, Bath.

French skier Ulmer is one of a small band
of extreme skiers
who feel they have outgrown normal skiing.

Normal ski trails are marked.
Signs tell everyone
how hard the different trails are.
Green circles are easy paths
for snow bunnies, or learners.
Blue squares are harder
but they can be skied by most good skiers.

Black diamonds are steep trails
for experts only.
Black diamonds offer plenty of excitement
for most people.
But not for Kristen Ulmer and friends.
To them, all marked trails look too tame.
They want to ski the impossible!

Black diamond trails are enough for most skiers.

What does impossible mean?
You can take your pick.
Some extreme skiers love
to ski off cliffs.
One extreme skier does backflips
off 20-metre cliffs.
Others like to ski
in the narrow openings between cliffs.

Another extreme skier is known
for skiing along thin strips of snow
that cut through the mountains of Italy.
He skis through passageways
with huge walls of rock on either side.
Sometimes the passageways
are no more than 3 metres wide.
One slip and he'll smash into the rocks.

He says:
'It's like skiing through a twisted cave.
The light is dim and far above you
and the rock walls blur
as you rocket past.'

Some enjoy the thrill of skiing
down a glacier in Antarctica.
Others choose to ski the summits
of huge mountains in Asia.
Extreme skiers live to prove
that what seems impossible
really can be done.

Skiing on a glacier.

Once a slope has been conquered,
extreme skiers often move on
to something else.
The idea is to find a place
that no one has ever skied before.

One famous extreme skier does that.
As he climbs cliffs
he is always searching
for something tougher.
He says:
'I spend all that energy
carrying my skis up there
and I don't want to waste it
just repeating the same old stuff.'

A top extreme skier from France
called Pierre Tardivel
feels the same way.
He says:
'I am not interested
if something has been done.
I want to know if it *can* be done.
That is the adventure.'

Skiing on Mount Everest.

He has skied nearly 50 firsts.
He was the first to ski
the south summit of Mount Everest.
At 9,600 metres,
that is higher than anyone on skis
has ever been.

Tardivel is an expert
at skiing down steep land.
Most black diamond trails have slopes
no steeper than 30 degrees.
Tardivel skis slopes of 45 to 60 degrees.
Imagine standing up straight
on such a steep slope.
At 45 degrees you could reach out
and touch the snow with your elbow!

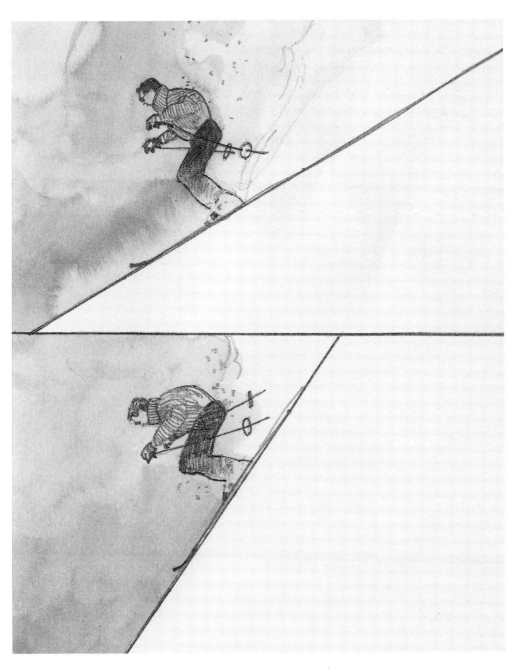

A black diamond slope (top) seems gentle
compared to the steep slopes tackled by extreme skiers
(bottom).

Tardivel takes his time
when he skis a new place.
He doesn't simply race down.
That would be suicide.
Instead, he picks his way along,
making one or two turns at a time.
He has to plan every move.
That way he can avoid ice and boulders
that are often found on the run.
Even so,
he usually slides 15 metres or more
before the edges of his skis
grip enough to stop.

People can die skiing the impossible.
Tardivel knows that better than most.
And he says he doesn't want to die.
There is a saying in extreme sports:
'Live and learn; learn or die.'
So Tardivel always climbs up a new run
before he skis down it.

Two French extreme skiers
died because they didn't climb up
a new run before they skied down it.

One took a helicopter to the summit
of a mountain in France.
He didn't know
there was black ice beneath the snow.
He slipped and fell to his death.

The other rode a ski lift to a summit
and walked over to a new place
he wanted to try.
He, too, fell to his death.
'Both were killed
because they started from the top,'
says Tardivel.

A skier jumps from a helicopter.

Why do extreme skiers risk their lives
in the first place?
To most of us,
it seems they must have a death wish.
But they deny that.
They say it isn't a matter
of courting death.
It's a matter of facing your fears
and overcoming them.

That's why one skier
became interested in the sport.
As a child, he liked to be pulled along
behind his father's snowmobile.
One day his father tried to take him
over a 1-metre jump.
The skier says:
'I chickened out and let go of the rope
right on the tip of the jump.
That's when I started
confronting my fears.'
The best way to do that, he found,
was by extreme skiing.

Conquering your fear
is not the same as losing your fear.
In fact, extreme skiers say
the fear is always there.
'You've got to have some fear
of what you're doing
or else you don't belong out there,'
declares American extreme skier
Dean Cummings.

All extreme skiers have some fear.

'We all know extreme skiing is dangerous,'
echoes Kristen Ulmer.
But she insists it's worth the risks.

For her, it's about
'the need to be the best you can be
and to express that through what you do.'
Also, Ulmer says,
extreme skiing helps you
believe in yourself.
You can become your own superhero.
You learn to have complete faith
in your abilities.
That faith, she says,
is very important
if you want to be an extreme skier.

Extreme skiers now compete
against each other every year
in the World Extreme Skiing Championship.
This event is not open to everyone.
You have to be well prepared.
You have to prove that you have skied
at least four extreme descents.
Skiers must be expert mountain climbers.
And they must be trained
in avoiding and surviving avalanches.

A skier takes part in the Championship.

In the championship,
the skiers are taken to the top
of some wild peak.
As they ski down,
judges grade them on style and difficulty.
If you win – great.
But just staying alive is also a success.

In 1993 a skier died
when the snow ledge he was on gave way.
For safety,
skiers must wear avalanche beacons.
That makes it possible for rescuers
to locate them and try to save them.

Dean Cummings once barely escaped death.
He was caught in an avalanche
and almost tumbled over a 33-metre cliff.
What did he think
about his brush with death?
It was a contest
between sheer fright and wild fun.
Cummings calls his experience
'the most incredible buzz
you could ever have.'

It is thoughts like this
that make Ulmer, Tardivel and Cummings
'extreme'.
The rest of us can find plenty of 'buzz'
on normal ski trails.